Mindful Scholar: Navigating Stress for Academic Success

From Overwhelm to Aces: The Ultimate Stress Transformation for Students

By: Deepika Kumari & Abhishek Keshri

ॐ गणेशाय नमः

ॐ सरस्वत्यै नमः

"Think Good,

Desire Good,

Intent Good,

Speak Good,

Act good ,

Listen Good"

Copywrite

Disclaimer

The information provided in this book is for general informational purposes only. It is not intended as legal, financial, or professional advice. Readers are advised to seek appropriate counsel or experts for specific situations.

Names, characters, places, and incidents are either the product of the author's imagination or are used fictitiously. Any resemblance to actual events or persons, living or dead, is entirely coincidental.

Expressions of Gratitude

Our sincere gratitude extends to Bhagwan/GOD for the profound inspiration, unwavering motivation, and immense strength that have guided us in crafting this transformative book. We also wish to extend heartfelt thanks to Bhagwan for orchestrating the timely assistance that propelled us to completion through various avenues. We are indebted to our cherished child, Advik, whose unyielding support, and boundless inspiration have been our guiding lights. We are humbled to express our deepest appreciation to our parents, teachers, and mentors whose nurturing guidance has illuminated our path. We extend our gratitude to all those who have directly or indirectly contributed to this book through their wisdom, motivation, and invaluable insights.

Preface: Unveiling the Pathway to Academic Brilliance

Introducing the Essence of the Book:

Embark on a transformative odyssey through **"Mindful Scholar: Navigating Stress for Academic Success."** This transformative volume is dedicated to empowering you to navigate the intricate terrain of stress, cultivate purpose-driven achievement, nurture meaningful relationships, envision a future of purpose, and infuse each moment with the enriching tapestry of mindfulness practices.

Chapter 1: Liberating Yourself from the Bonds of Student Stress

Revelations of Student Stress Complexity:

Peer into the intricate web of stress factors interwoven into the tapestry of student life. Traverse through the layers of stress's impact on academic performance, mental equilibrium, and personal well-being. Immerse yourself in the invitation to embark on a voyage towards skillful stress management through mindfulness.

Chapter 2: The Mindful Arsenal

Mindfulness as the Keystone of Stress Mastery:

Unveil the cornerstone of effective stress management – mindfulness. Delve into the scientific underpinnings that underscore its cognitive and emotional virtues. Illuminate the empowerment that mindfulness confers upon students, enabling him to navigate stress with resilience and amplify his cognitive capacities.

Chapter 3: Navigating Stress Through the Prism of Mindful Approaches

Exploring a Palette of Mindful Approaches:

Embark on a discovery of versatile mindfulness practices tailored to the distinctive needs of students. Find lucid guidance on engaging in mindfulness exercises, ranging from the art of mindful breathing to profound body scans. Be prompted to seamlessly integrate mindfulness into your daily routines.

Chapter 4: Transforming Stress into Triumph

Chronicles of Triumph Amidst Stress:

Unfold narratives of students who have harnessed stress as a catalyst for his academic accomplishments. Demystify the art of reframing stress and its power to shape attitudes and outcomes. Equip yourself with actionable strategies to channel stress as a dynamic catalyst for personal growth and achievement.

Chapter 5: Mastery of the Examination Arena through Mindful Mastery

Deciphering the Nuances of Examination Stress:

Probe the distinct stress facets intricately linked with examinations and evaluations. Reveal mindfulness techniques that empower you to surmount pre-exam anxiety, elevate performance, and amplify memory retention and cognitive prowess.

Chapter 6: Mastery of Time: Unveiling the Art of Productivity through Mindfulness

Traversing the Labyrinth of Time Management:

Confront the labyrinthine challenge of time management faced by students. Engage with mindfulness-infused strategies that propel productivity while dismantling procrastination. Develop a harmonious study routine that nurtures both accomplishments and well-being.

Chapter 7: Cultivating Resilience and Nurturing Mental Flourishing

Unpacking the Significance of Emotional Resilience:

Examine the pivotal role of emotional resilience in the student journey. Equip yourself with tools to navigate setbacks, failures, and the scholastic pressures with grace and fortitude. Uncover the intricate interplay of mindfulness, self-care, and the flourishing of mental well-being.

Chapter 8: Navigating Interpersonal Bonds with Mindful Poise

Spotlighting the Interpersonal Dimensions of Student Life:

Illuminate the rich tapestry of interpersonal relationships within the realm of student existence. Present communication techniques fortified by mindfulness that enhance effective collaboration and teamwork. Explore strategies for conflict resolution through the prism of mindful awareness.

Chapter 9: The Expedition Ahead: Mindfulness as an Eternal Companion

Transcending the Classroom: Mindfulness as Universal Wisdom:

Transcend the confines of the academic realm and explore the universal application of mindfulness. Probe its role in shaping personal values, aspirations, and the holistic growth of life. Embrace the inspiration to continue the mindfulness journey beyond academic horizons.

Chapter 10: Embracing the Unknown Future with Mindful Certainty

Stepping into the Abyss: Navigating the Uncharted Waters of Tomorrow

In this concluding chapter, we explore how mindfulness can be our guiding star as we confront the uncertainty of what lies ahead. Through the mentorship of Professor Evelyn and the lessons learned in stress management, achievement, relationships, resilience, and mental flourishing, we equip ourselves with the tools needed to navigate life's twists and turns with poise and assurance.

Conclusion: The Mindful Voyage- Unleashing Empowerment Through Presence

Synthesis of Key Lessons:

Weave together the profound lessons and insights cultivated throughout the book. Emphasize the metamorphic potency of mindfulness within the academic landscape. Invite readers to embrace mindfulness as an enduring tool for sustainable success and fulfillment.

Summary: Embrace the Symphony of Empowerment

A Journey of Revelation:

Embark on an expedition of enlightenment, empowerment, and transformation as you immerse yourself in the symphony of mindful existence. Let the journey through academics be defined by wisdom, expansion, and the clarion call to act.

Table of Contents

5. The Unveiling of Mindful Relationships

Chapter 9: The Expedition Ahead: Mindfulness as an Eternal Companion

1. Embarking on the Continuation
2. The Ripple Effect of Mindfulness
3. A Commencement, Not an End
4. Beyond the Classroom: Mindfulness as a Guiding Star
5. Mindfulness: Navigating the Seas of Life with Purpose and Clarity

Chapter 10: Embracing the Unknown Future with Mindful Certainty

1. The Horizon of Impossibilities
2. The Palette of Mindful Vision
3. The Authority of Intention
4. The Choreography of Goals and Present Endeavors
5. Gateway to Flexibility
6. The Mindful Mosaic of Tomorrow

Conclusion: The Mindful Voyage- Unleashing Empowerment Through Presence

1. The Epitome of Wisdom's Culmination
2. The Potency of Present Empowerment

Summary: Embrace the Symphony of Empowerment

1. A Voyage of Unveiling and Growth
2. A Symphony of Empowerment and Transformation
3. Answering the Call to Ignite Your Empowerment
4. Tools & Tips

Introduction: A Dynamic Classroom and an Enigmatic Discovery

Nestled within the vibrant tapestry of academia, where the corridors pulsed with the ceaseless rhythm of students dashing between lectures, assignments, and the ceaseless pursuit of excellence, Alex, an ambitious scholar, found himself swept into the whirlwind. Echoing footsteps resonated through the hallways, and the air hummed with an undeniable tension, seeping into every facet of Alex's academic journey.

Amidst the academic fervor, where stress and pressure held sway, a fascinating revelation was poised to unfurl—a revelation that would reshape the trajectory of Alex's educational odyssey and extend its influence far beyond.

As you embark on the pages of "Mindful Scholar: Navigating Stress for Academic Success," be prepared to step into the shoes of Alex and immerse yourself in the academic realm as experienced through His eyes. Traverse the landscape laden with expectations, the throbbing pulse of examination days, and the intricate tightrope walk of balancing ambition with well-being.

Yet, amidst this tumultuous backdrop, emerges a glimmer of hope—a mentor, sagacious and compassionate, who introduces Alex to a transformative paradigm: **MINDFULNESS**. The potency of mindfulness radiates as a guiding beacon, offering a means to navigate the storm of stress and attain crystalline clarity amidst academic turbulence.

Embrace this journey that is as much a quest for scholastic excellence as it is a search for internal tranquility. Encounter the art of stress mastery, the scientific tapestry of resilience, and the profound resonance of mindfulness within a student's realm. Through the undulating contours of Alex's narrative, you will unearth the enigmatic alchemy that transforms overwhelm into the brilliance of academic accomplishment.

Whether you are a student navigating the labyrinth of academic challenges, an educator shepherding young minds, or an individual intrigued by the labyrinthine landscape of academic stress, this volume invites you to partake in an immersive expedition—a journey from being encumbered to being empowered, from being overwhelmed to achieving "aces," and above all, from discord to serene equilibrium.

Dive into the pages of "Mindful Scholar," wherein the tale of one scholar's metamorphosis mirrors the potential inherent within us all to flourish amid the rigors of academic pursuits.

Chapter 1: Liberating Yourself from the Grip of Student Stress

The Whirlwind of Academic Life

Within the heart of Crestmont University, where dreams merged seamlessly with deadlines, aspirations entwined with anxieties, and the scent of potential intermingled with the tang of stress, resided Alex—a relentless seeker of wisdom and an unwavering scholar. Crestmont was more than a mere institution; it was a universe in its own right, alive with students racing against time, racing against expectations, and racing to establish His unique marks.

As dawn's earliest light brushed the campus in hues of gold, the symphony of hurried footsteps echoed through the corridors. The scene pulsated with energy and intention, yet beneath this bustling exterior, a common thread wove through every student's narrative—stress.

Amid this academic kaleidoscope, Alex stood as a protagonist on a voyage of self-discovery. Lectures melded into labs, and assignments seamlessly intertwined with exams, forging an unbroken whirlwind of academic responsibilities. Striving to balance textbooks, timetables, social connections, and study sessions, Alex's journey mirrored that of countless students who had tread upon Crestmont's paths.

The Burden of Expectations

Within this panorama of activity, Professor Evelyn emerged as a figure of enigma—a mentor whose influence transcended the confines of the classroom. With silver hair framing a serene visage and eyes brimming with the sagacity borne of years within academia, Evelyn epitomized poise.

One brisk morning, as autumn leaves danced upon the breeze, Alex stood at the threshold of Professor Evelyn's domain. The air crackled with anticipation, for within those four walls lay the promise of insight, guidance, and perhaps a remedy for the escalating burden of stress.

As the dialogue unfolded, Evelyn listened with an empathetic ear, attuned not just to the words but also to the cadence of the heart behind him. "Professor, the pressure is relentless," Alex confessed. "The deadlines, the expectations—each day feels like an unending battle."

Evelyn nodded in understanding, and with a gentle smile, began to recount a tale—a tale of His own student days, when the weight of expectations threatened to engulf him.

"My final year," Evelyn reminisced, "The culmination of years of toil. Yet, as the finish line neared, so did the undercurrent of anxiety. The exams loomed like towering peaks, and I carried the weight of the world upon my shoulders."

With each communication, the bond between Alex and Evelyn deepened. The narrative was not a mere recollection; it was a lifeline, a bridge spanning generations and experiences. It points out that the struggle was not solitary, and within it lay the germination of personal evolution.

"Alex," Evelyn intoned, fixing His gaze, "Stress is a formidable adversary, yet it can also be a catalyst for transformation. Just as a sculptor molds clay, stress shapes us. The question is, will you allow it to sculpt you into something more resilient, or will you let it fracture you?"

A Path Revealed

In those moments, as the wisdom of years entangled with the curiosity of youth, a spark ignited within Alex. The voyage to comprehend stress, tame its dominance, and ultimately flourish amid its turbulence became a journey of profound significance.

****

As this chapter fold up, you will traverse not just Crestmont's halls, but also the corridors of your own encounters. You will journey alongside Alex, witnessing the zeniths and nadirs, the conquests and tribulations that form the mosaic of a student's life.

This chapter is not a mere segment—it is a portal into the realm of academic stress and how mindfulness can reshape it. Brace yourself for an odyssey that interlaces narratives, revelations, and pragmatic tools into a tapestry of self-discovery and elevation. Welcome to the path of the Mindful Scholar.

Key Lessons from Chapter 1

a. Stress is an inseparable companion of academic life.

b. The burden of expectations can be weighty.

c. Stress can be a catalyst for personal growth.

d. Mentorship and shared experiences provide invaluable perspectives.

Action Steps:

a. Reflect on personal experiences with academic stress.

b. Identify specific stress triggers and the emotions they evoke.

c. Seek inspiration from mentors or individuals who have confronted similar challenges— gather insights from His stories.

d. Initiate a journal to chronicle thoughts and emotions linked to stress and expectations.

Chapter 2: The Mindful Arsenal

Embarking on Mindfulness: Guided by Radiant Wisdom

Alex stood at the crossroads of curiosity and transformation. Reverberating in His mind were Professor Evelyn's words from His previous encounter: , "Stress is a formidable adversary, yet it can also be a catalyst for transformation. Just as a sculptor molds clay, stress shapes us. The question is, will you allow it to sculpt you into something more resilient, or will you let it fracture you?"

As the sun painted the campus in gilded hues, Alex found himself immersed in a stack of books within the university library. However, this time, a newfound curiosity kindled—a curiosity to fathom stress, to decode its mechanisms, and to reveal the instruments capable of transmuting it from adversary to ally.

The library, a bastion of wisdom, seemed to harbor enigmatic truths awaiting revelation. In the aisles, Alex stumbled upon a treasure trove of books centered on mindfulness—a concept that had long fascinated him but remained unexplored until now.

The Science Behind Mindfulness: Rewiring Resilient Neural Pathways

With each turned page, a world of understanding unfurled. Mindfulness was more than a mere catchphrase; it was a discipline, a philosophy, a way of existing. The deeper Alex delved, the clearer it became that mindfulness transcended mere relaxation; it entailed cultivating resilience, enhancing concentration, and navigating life's tempests with grace.

The scientific underpinning of mindfulness was captivating. It was not a fleeting idea; it entailed rewiring the brain. It involved transforming ingrained reactions into conscious responses, forging new neural pathways divergent from the realm of stress and anxiety. The brain, as it turned out, was astonishingly adaptable, and mindfulness served as the sculptor's tool.

Professor Evelyn's Insights: In a subsequent conversation later that week, Professor Evelyn delved deeper into the science. "Alex," he conveyed, "mindfulness isn't solely about stress management; it transforms our perception of it. The amygdala, a gland present in our brain, responsible for the fight-or-flight response, becomes less reactive. Meanwhile, the prefrontal cortex, the seat of rational thinking, strengthens. This creates a buffer—a realm between stimulus and reaction. In that space, your power to choose, to respond mindfully, resides."

Energized by newfound enthusiasm, Alex embarked on a journey of mindfulness practice. Breathing exercises metamorphosed into portals to tranquility, body scans unveiled concealed pockets of tension, and guided visualizations transported him to serene landscapes within His mind's eye.

The Voyage Inward

Amidst Crestmont's serene courtyard, beneath the shade of an ancient, wise tree, perched a solitary bench. Here, Alex discovered His sanctuary, a realm where he embarked on journeys within—an expedition into the realm of mindfulness.

Eyes gently closed, 3 to 5 deep breaths taken, and Alex was enveloped by a wave of serenity. Amid life's cacophony, this space offered stillness. Every inhalation became a tether to the present moment, each exhalation an unravelling of stress. The breath, often overlooked, morphed into a thread knitting the external world to His internal landscape.

Professor Evelyn's Insights: In a subsequent dialogue, Professor Evelyn illuminated the breath's significance. "The breath, Alex, is your constant companion, a bridge between your external and internal realms. Focusing on your breath aligns you with the rhythm of now. In that alignment lies the power to disengage from the whirlwind of thoughts, worries, and stressors."

Clarity Amidst Turmoil

Weeks transformed into months, and the practice of mindfulness seamlessly wove itself into Alex's daily routine. Although stress occasionally knocked at the door—exams loomed, assignments accumulated—a newfound shield stood ready, forged through mindfulness.

One evening, as the sun's golden glow surrendered to the horizon, Alex found himself seated on the bench beneath the wise, ancient tree. Exams loomed ever closer, and while nervous anticipation fluttered, an unprecedented tranquility coexisted.

Professor Evelyn's Insights: In His final discussion of the semester, Professor Evelyn unveiled a profound insight. "Alex," he shared, "mindfulness isn't about eradicating stress; it's about metamorphosing your relationship with it. Stress is akin to a passing storm—it comes, then it dissipates. Yet through mindfulness, you become the steadfast anchor. Amidst the storm, clarity emerges, empowering you to navigate challenges."

As the semester drew to a close, Alex contemplated His journey. What had begun as a quest for tools to cope with stress had transmuted into an expedition of self-discovery. Mindfulness transcended technique: it was an ethos, a lens through which life could be savored with depth and presence.

Key Lessons from Chapter 2:

    a.   Mindfulness is a scientifically grounded strategy for managing stress.

    b.   It encompasses rewiring the brain for resilience and conscious response.

    c.   Practices such as focused breathing, body scans, and visualizations tether us to the present moment.

    d.   Mindfulness reconfigures our interaction with stress, nurturing lucidity, and conscious choice.

Action Steps:

    a.   Commence your day with a succinct mindful breathing session.

    b.   Dedicate time to conducting a body scan, exploring sensations across your body.

c. Experiment with guided visualizations
    to experience interludes of calm.

d. Cultivate the practice of mindful
    walking during interludes, savoring
    every step and sensation.

Chapter 3: Navigating Stress Through the Prism of Mindful Approaches

Breathing into Serenity: The Art of Mindful Breathing Techniques

The flux of academic life converged with the introspective journey of self-discovery, Alex's exploration of mindfulness. Professor Evelyn's sagacious counsel echoed like a guiding melody, propelling him toward a voyage into the treasure trove of mindfulness methods.

Amidst the bustling tapestry of campus life, Alex discovered solace in a quiet corner of the student center—a haven of tranquility amidst the whirlwind of obligations. Empowered by the knowledge of mindfulness's transformative potential, he embarked on an expedition into the universe of mindful breathing.

The Breath as an Anchor

Sitting in serene comfort, eyes softly shut, Alex's focus turned to His breath, Inhale and Exhale. The breath evolved into a steadfast ally, grounding His attention. Each inhalation extended an invitation to the present, while each exhalation released the grip of concerns.

As moments flowed by, an aura of serenity enfolded him. The turbulent realm of thoughts began to still, and within the rhythmic cadence of breath, a sanctuary emerged—untouched by the maelstrom of academic pressures.

Professor Evelyn's Insights: In a discussion as gentle as a breeze, Professor Evelyn illuminated the profound essence of mindful breathing. "Alex," he conveyed, "the breath serves as a bridge, linking your internal and external worlds. When you center your awareness on your breath, you tether yourself to the here and now. It's a tool ever at your disposal, offering solace amidst life's tempests."

Embodied Awareness: The Transformative Magic of Body Scans

As days transitioned into weeks, Alex's journey into mindfulness deepened. His exploration led him to a novel technique—the body scan. Amid the hush of early mornings, he reclined in comfort, ready to traverse His body's intricate landscape.

Guided by the gentle rhythm of breath, Alex directed His consciousness to distinct body regions. Starting from His toes, he ascended, sensing nuances, tensions, and subtle undercurrents. With each passing instant, a profound awareness burgeoned—an awareness of His body's narratives, its whispers, and its sagacity.

Professor Evelyn's Insights: In a dialogue resembling a poetic unveiling, Professor Evelyn emphasized the significance of the body scan.

"Alex," he imparted, "the body is a repository of experiences. By scanning it with mindful attention, you unlock its messages with regular practice. You invite the release of tensions, forging a harmonious rapport between mind and body."

Visualization and Metamorphosis: Guided Visualizations

As the semester marched forward, Alex delved deeper into mindfulness's arsenal, discovering the art of guided visualizations. Enveloped by Professor Evelyn's voice, he embarked on inner odysseys to tranquil landscapes, distant shores, and serene woodlands.

In one visualization, he stood at the edge of a serene lake. The water mirrored the heavens, and with each breath, a sensation of expansion, of merging with the expanse, enveloped him. The burdens of exams and assignments seemed to dissolve in the tranquil ripples of the lake.

Professor Evelyn's Insights: Amidst a conversation akin to a romantic dance of words, Professor Evelyn shared His reflections on visualizations. "Alex," he conveyed, "visualizations transcend the bounds of thought. They ferry you to realms that revive your inherent tranquility. Through him, you unearth an inner wellspring of calm, accessible whenever needed."

Walking with Consciousness: The Craft of Mindful Walking

As the tapestry of academia unfolded, Alex ventured further into mindfulness in motion—the practice of mindful walking. Amidst Crestmont's botanical haven, he treads mindfully, relishing each sensation, each step.

With every stride, Alex was attuned to the rhythm of movement, the tactile encounter, and the gentle sway of leaves on the breeze. It was a choreography of awareness—a dance that embraced not solely the external universe but the universe within.

Professor Evelyn's Insights: In a discussion reminiscent of a ballet of thoughts, Professor Evelyn illuminated the profundities of mindful walking. "Alex," he mused, "walking embodies life's essence. When you walk mindfully, you dedicate full presence to each step. It's a reminder that existence unfurls step by step, and within that unfurling resides a realm of experience."

Key Lessons from Chapter 3:

a. Mindful breathing serves as a portal to the serene, granting respite from stress.

b. Body scans nurture consciousness of bodily sensations and tensions.

c. Guided visualizations transport us to tranquil landscapes, nurturing tranquility.

d. Mindful walking connects us to the cadence of movement and the universe around us.

Action Steps:

a. Inaugurate your day with a brief mindful breathing ritual.
b. Dedicate moments to a comprehensive body scan, exploring sensations across your body.
c. Embark on guided visualizations for intervals of tranquility.
d. In your breaks, embrace the practice of mindful walking, cherishing every step and sensation.

Chapter 4: Transforming Stress into Triumph

A Tale of Dual Perspectives

The fabric of academic existence intricately woven with threads of self-discovery, Alex's odyssey through mindfulness pressed onward. Professor Evelyn's sagacity had evolved into a compass, deftly steering him through the labyrinthine corridors of stress. As the days seamlessly transformed into weeks, a transformation was unfurling—a shift of outlook.

Upon a particularly overcast morning, Alex discovered himself within the tranquil courtyard of the university. The wise, ancient tree's bench beckoned, inviting a moment of introspection. Professor Evelyn's narratives and insights intertwined with His personal encounters, compelling Alex to question the essence of stress itself.

The Struggle and Its Gilded Lining

Amidst this contemplative trance, Alex's reflections meandered back to the outset of His voyage. The ceaseless deadlines, the pursuit of excellence—it had been akin to an unwavering conflict. Yet, within the conflict, he found glimmers of growth—instances of resilience that had forged a stronger self.

Professor Evelyn's Illumination: In a conversation reminiscent of an interlude with time itself, Professor Evelyn highlighted the paradox of stress. "Alex," he conveyed, "stress isn't an adversary; it stands as an ally. It mirrors a sculptor's chisel, shaping you. The very trials that appear formidable are the building blocks of advancement. When your perspective shifts, stress metamorphoses into a catalyst for accomplishment."

From Overwhelm to Empowerment

Empowered by this novel viewpoint, Alex embarked on a journey to transmute stress into a wellspring of strength. No longer was he mere bystanders to stress's influence; now, he stood as alchemists of His own experiences. Exams were no longer towering obstacles; he had transmuted into steppingstones for personal growth. Assignments ceased to be burdens; he revealed himself as avenues to exhibit his expertise.

With each deliberate choice, stress ceased to be a burden and emerged as an impetus—an impetus propelling him forward, intensifying His resolve, and honing His concentration. Days marred by overwhelm were replaced by days marked by intentional dominion.

Professor Evelyn's Discourse: In a dialogue resembling a symphony of wisdom, Professor Evelyn elaborated on the concept of ownership. "Alex," he remarked, "stress relinquishes its hold when you grasp the reins. The objective is not to obliterate stress but to adeptly navigate its currents. As you face challenges purposefully, you harness the energy of stress for your aspirations."

Extracting Diamonds from Pressure

One twilight, with the campus bathed in the golden embrace of sunset, Alex found himself engaged in a conversation with a fellow student. Amidst laughter and camaraderie, the topic shifted to impending exams. To His surprise, instead of the customary collective sighs, Alex felt an internal smile blossoming.

Guided by His newfound perspective, he shared insights—how stress was not a nemesis but a collaborator in His journey. He recounted instances when pressure had led to discoveries, when deadlines had refined His skills, and when the intensity of exams had unveiled His capacities.

Professor Evelyn's Sharing: During a fireside discussion that resembled a congregation of kindred souls, Professor Evelyn shared His musings. "Alex," he remarked, "when you disclose your transformation, you become a guiding light. You demonstrate that stress can be molded, transmuted into accomplishments. Through reshaping the narrative, you foster a culture that embraces challenges rather than dreads him."

The Blossoming of the Mindful Scholar

As the semester neared its conclusion, Alex found himself at the juncture of His expedition. The transformation was palpable evolving from a student ensnared by stress to a mindful scholar channeling its vigor. While the whirlwind of academic life remained unaltered, His dance within it had undergone a profound alteration.

Guided by Professor Evelyn's counsel and armed with the tools of mindfulness, Alex had redefined the narrative. Stress had shifted from a liability to an asset. He had uncovered that within the crucible of stress, the unprocessed materials of growth lay- the alchemy of accomplishment.

Key Lessons from Chapter 4:

a. Stress can be morphed from a nemesis into an ally.
b. Challenges and pressures serve as platforms for growth and resilience.
c. A change in perspective empowers us to harness stress's energy for our ambitions.
d. Sharing personal transformations can kindle a culture that embraces challenges.

Action Steps:

a. Reflect on previous challenges that have catalyzed personal development.

b. Alter your viewpoint on stress, recognizing it as a wellspring of energy and advancement.

c. Confront challenges with intent, utilizing stress as a propellant toward achievement.

d. Share your metamorphosis with others, igniting a culture where empowered outlooks prevail.

Chapter 5: Mastery of the Examination Arena through Mindful Mastery

Decoding the Landscape of Examination Anxieties

The pursuit of knowledge intertwined seamlessly with life's rhythm, Alex's voyage through mindfulness upsurge. Professor Evelyn's wisdom had illuminated avenues through stress, but a looming tempest adorned the horizon—the exams.

With the semester's end drawing near, the campus hummed with a blend of anticipation and anxiety. Clusters of students huddled together, exchanging notes, strategies, and the distinct resonance of stress. Amidst the commotion, Alex experienced the palpitations of exam anxiety;

however, a fresh kind of serenity emerged amidst the chaos—a serenity born of mindfulness.

Mindful Examination Strategies: The Art of Preparation, Presence, and Performance

Seated beneath the wise, ancient tree's shade, Alex's thoughts navigated a labyrinth of contemplation. The impending exams were not mere evaluations; he was a stage for his newfound mindfulness prowess to radiate. Guided by Professor Evelyn's expertise, he had nurtured a mindful toolkit—a toolkit imbued with the power to transmute anxiety into composed concentration.

Professor Evelyn's Illumination: In a discourse akin to the prelude of a grand symphony, Professor Evelyn unveiled a mindful exam strategy. "Alex," he shared, "preparation, presence, and performance—these are the triadic movements of your symphony. Preparation serves as your bedrock, presence as your conductor, and performance as your magnum opus. Through mindfulness, you'll navigate each movement with poise."

The Bedrock of Preparation

In the days leading up to the exams, Alex found himself encircled by mountains of textbooks, annotated notes, and study guides. Yet, a transformational shift was evident in His approach. Mindfulness was not reserved solely for meditation sessions; it was a constant companion throughout His journey of study.

As he delved into his studies, Alex applied mindful focus—a state where the mind was wholly immersed in the task at hand. Every word, every equation transformed into a gateway to mindfulness. He discovered that mindful studying was not about quantity; it was about depth— about engrossing oneself fully in the material.

Professor Evelyn's Insight: In a dialogue reminiscent of an orchestration of wisdom, Professor Evelyn expounded upon mindful preparation. "Alex," he conveyed, "mindful study is a dance with the subject matter. When you are completely present, your comprehension deepens. The bond between mindfulness and studying isn't linear; it's transformative."

Conductor of Presence

As the eve of the exams neared, Alex found himself

on the precipice of presence. Seated in the library's quiet alcove, he embarked on a mindful breathing exercise, grounding himself in the immediate moment, Inhale and Exhale. With each breath, he relinquished past ruminations and future apprehensions, embracing the present fully.

As he entered the exam room, the commotion of students and the weight of expectations took a backseat to the symphony of presence. Mindful breaths acted as anchors, and each question morphed into a note within the exam's composition. Distractions faded away, leaving only the conductor of presence guiding every movement.

Professor Evelyn's Perspective: In a conversation akin to a harmonious duet, Professor Evelyn offered His insights on exam presence. "Alex," he shared, "presence is your antidote to anxiety. When anchored in the present, worries cease to sweep you away. Every question becomes an opportunity to apply your knowledge mindfully."

The Magnum Opus of Performance

As the final exam drew to a close, Alex found himself at the summit of His journey. The tempest of exams had passed, leaving behind a trail of answered questions and the resonance of mindfulness. He discovered that the essence of mindful performance transcended mere perfect scores; it was the fusion of endeavor and presence.

Professor Evelyn's Reflection: In a conversation that felt like a crescendo, Professor Evelyn pondered mindful performance. "Alex," he imparted, "your performance is not confined to its outcome. It is characterized by the intention woven into every response; the presence infused into every question. Through mindfulness, you craft a symphony of endeavor and elegance."

Key Lessons from Chapter 5:

a. A mindful exam strategy involves preparation, presence, and performance.

b.   Mindful studying entails wholehearted engagement with the material, deepening understanding.

c.   Presence during exams quells anxiety and magnifies concentration on each question.

d.   Mindful performance hinges on merging effort and presence, transcending results.

Action Steps:

a.   Infuse mindfulness into your study regimen for heightened engagement.

b.   Practice mindful breathing prior to entering the exam room to ground yourself in the present.

c.   Confront each exam question with unwavering presence, focusing solely on the query at hand.

d.   Reflect on your exam experience, emphasizing effort and presence over outcomes.

Chapter 6: Mastery of Time: Unveiling the Art of Productivity through Mindfulness

Cracking the Code of Time Mastery

The academic avenues merged seamlessly with the byways of life; Alex stood poised on the brink of a new realm: the realm of time mastery. Guided by the sagacity of Professor Evelyn, this chapter was destined to unravel the enigma of wielding time through the prism of mindfulness – a skill that would amplify Alex's productivity and metamorphose His days into a symphony of achievements.

The Dance of Efficiency and Presence

As the sun cast its tender rays upon the campus, Alex embarked on a journey of profound revelation – a voyage that would traverse the labyrinth of tasks, deadlines, and aspirations. The pursuit of productivity was not to be divorced from the domain of presence; rather, the two were to be entwined in a graceful ballet, much like dancers harmonizing in exquisite synchrony.

Morning Rituals: The Gateway to Empowered Days

In the serenity of the dawn, Alex unearthed the magical potency of morning rituals. Under the aegis of Professor Evelyn's counsel, he imbibed each action with mindful awareness. From the leisurely inhalation of invigorating air to the deliberate sips of a revitalizing elixir, every instant evolved into a musical note in the symphony of mornings, establishing the cadence for a day brimming with purposeful engagement.

Nugget of Wisdom from Professor Evelyn: In a conversation reminiscent of a sunrise of wisdom,

Professor Evelyn imparted insights about morning rituals. "Alex," he conveyed, "the break of dawn sets the tone for the day ahead. By infusing each action with mindfulness, you lay the cornerstone for enhanced productivity. Morning rituals are the conduits that connect the repose of slumber with the dynamism of wakefulness."

Mindful Work: Transmuting Tasks into Triumphs

With the ascent of the sun, Alex transitioned seamlessly into the bustling sphere of work. Armed with the armamentarium of mindful wisdom, he embarked on a journey of conscious labor. Rather than surrendering to the vortex of autopilot, he embraced the virtue of mindful concentration – a state where each task was approached with intent and unwavering focus.

During meetings, Alex practiced the art of present listening, allowing the dialogues of colleagues to paint vivid tapestries in His consciousness. The outcome: Profound connections, enriched dialogues, and a mosaic of productivity adorned with mindful brushstrokes.

Pearl of Insight from Professor Evelyn: In a discourse echoing the symphony of productivity, Professor Evelyn shared His musings about mindful work. "Alex," he remarked, "mindful work transcends the myth of multitasking. It entails investing yourself wholly in every task but one at a time, immersing in a state of flow. Your work metamorphoses into an embodiment of mindful presence."

Mastering Concentration: The Alchemy of Monotasking

Amidst assignments and projects, Alex confronted the formidable adversary of distractions. Be it the siren call of social media notifications, the clamor of buzzing phones, or the meandering paths of wandering thoughts, hey waged a war against distraction. Yet, equipped with the wisdom bestowed by Professor Evelyn, he unraveled the art of hyper focus mono-tasking – the discipline of dedicating undivided focus to a solitary task.

By virtue of mindful determination, he allocated specific intervals for focused work, barricading against distractions and affording His mind the luxury of absolute absorption. The fruit of His endeavors was an elevated level of focus, a surge in productivity, and an unprecedented mastery over time.

Time Alchemy Techniques: A Pantheon of Mindful Tools

As the day unfurled its tapestry, Alex delved deeper into the treasure trove of mindful time management. He embraced techniques that seemed to warp the fabric of time itself –

techniques that heightened efficiency and propelled productivity to zenith.

Time Blocking: Infused with mindful intent, he partitioned His day into blocks of focused time, aligning each block with specific tasks. This practice not only engendered heightened concentration but also acted as a bulwark against the incursion of time-devouring diversions.

The Pomodoro Technique: Armed with a timer and a spirit of mindfulness, Alex embraced the Pomodoro Technique. Work intervals were punctuated by brief intermissions, fostering mental rejuvenation, and circumventing the pitfalls of burnout.

Prioritization: Guided by the beacon of mindful insight, Alex ascended the zenith of prioritization. No longer entangled by the dilemma of myriad tasks, he sifted through the labyrinth of obligations, channeling His energy into the activities of paramount import.

Learning through Contemplation: The Midday Reverie

As the sun reached its zenith, casting intricate patterns of light and shadow, Alex incorporated a new ritual into His routine: the midday reverie. This ritual was an oasis amidst the hustle and bustle — an interval for recalibration, reflection, and consolidation of the day's voyage.

Beneath the venerable canopy of the wise old tree, he sat with journal in hand, embarking on a journey of introspection. What tasks had been executed mindfully? What obstacles had been surmounted with equanimity? What insights had been gleaned? Through the prism of mindful reflection, Alex nurtured self-awareness and steeled himself for the latter half of the day.

Evening Reflections: Navigating the Twilight Hours

As the sun dipped beneath the horizon, Alex's focus shifted to the evening, where the practice of reflection awaited. This was a ritual that cast a retrospective gaze on the day's symphony. Professor Evelyn's teachings guided him to identify moments of accomplishment, connection, and evolution, and to transcribe him in the journal of His thoughts.

In the tranquil embrace of twilight, Alex's reflections took form, each stroke imbued with a palette of gratitude. This ritual served not only to draw the day to a close but also to illuminate the path for further mindful growth.

The Art of Transition: Evening Rituals

As the day's responsibilities ebbed away, Alex embraced the art of evening rituals. These rituals were mindful bridges that spanned the chasm between work and leisure. With purposeful motions – the lighting of a tranquilizing candle, the inhalation of soothing fragrances, and the gentle unfurling of pages in a book – he transitioned seamlessly from the realm of labor to that of leisure.

Professor Evelyn's Epiphany: In a discourse reminiscent of a breeze of tranquility, Professor Evelyn conveyed His insights on evening rituals. "Alex," he pronounced, "transitional rituals are akin to thresholds between chapters. By infusing him with mindfulness, you carve out a sanctuary for restful reprieve. These rituals pave the way for mindful rejuvenation."

Action Steps:

    a.   Embrace morning rituals as the bedrock of a day suffused with mindful presence.

b.   Indulge in mindful focus during work, treating each task as a note in the opus of productivity.

c.   Conquer distractions through the power of monotasking, dedicating unwavering attention to singular endeavors.

d.   Harness time-alchemy techniques like time blocking and the Pomodoro Technique for maximal efficiency.

e.   Participate in the midday reverie, contemplating the day's voyage and nurturing self-awareness.

f.   Engage in evening reflections, documenting instances of accomplishment and evolution.

g.   Envelop your evening with rituals that facilitate seamless transition from work to leisure, nurturing mindful rejuvenation.

****

As the curtain descends upon this chapter, engrave upon your consciousness that time is an easel awaiting your mindful strokes. By suffusing every fleeting moment with presence, intent, and design, you transmute quotidian days into resplendent symphonies of productivity. The sagacity shared by Professor Evelyn has equipped you with the implements to navigate time's labyrinth, and now the mantle falls to you, to orchestrate your days with the melody of accomplishment and the harmony of engaged mindfulness.

Chapter 7: Nurturing Resilience and Fostering Mental Flourishing: A Journey Within

Unveiling the Inner Landscape of Resilience

With the converged of knowledge and wisdom, Alex embarked on a new odyssey: the exploration of resilience and mental flourishing. Guided by the luminous insights of Professor Evelyn, this chapter delved into the profound realm of emotional strength, imparting the tools to weather life's storms and cultivate a garden of mental thriving.

The Foundation of Resilience: Embracing the Storms

As the sun painted the canvas of the campus with hues of gold, Alex embarked on a voyage to understand the very essence of resilience.

Professor Evelyn's guidance unveiled resilience as a sanctuary amidst life's tempests, a fortress forged not through invulnerability, but through the courage to acknowledge vulnerability.

It was through the tapestry of struggles and adversities that resilience found its fertile ground. The journey of mindfulness, replete with its stressors, achievements, relationships, and future visions, became the crucible in which resilience was shaped. With every challenge overcome, with every setback navigated, Alex's emotional armor grew stronger, empowering him to emerge from the crucible unbroken.

Navigating Emotional Landscapes: The Gift of Mindful Awareness

Amidst the myriad emotions that coursed through the tapestry of His journey, Alex learned that mindful awareness was the compass guiding him through emotional landscapes. Rather than succumbing to the torrents of emotion, he discovered the power to observe and acknowledge feelings without judgment, to be present with the ebbs and flows of his emotional tides.

In moments of stress, mindful breathing became the anchor that prevented him from being swept away by the storm. Through this practice, he harnessed the reins of His emotional state, transforming turmoil into a platform for growth. It was through this awareness that resilience was cultivated, allowing him to bounce back from challenges with newfound strength.

Pearls of Wisdom from Professor Evelyn: In a dialogue that echoed like a soothing melody, Professor Evelyn shared insights on emotional resilience. "Alex," he conveyed, "emotions are not adversaries to be conquered; they are allies to be understood; they are like an encrypted message. Through mindful awareness, you gain the power to navigate your inner landscape with grace and strength."

Cultivating a Garden of Mental Flourishing: The Mind-Body Connection

As the sun traversed its celestial arc, Alex embarked on the path of mental flourishing – a journey intertwined with the mind-body connection. Professor Evelyn's teachings illuminated the symbiotic relationship between thoughts, emotions, and physical well-being.

He discovered that the thoughts he nurtured were seeds sown in the garden of His mind. Positive affirmations and self-compassion became the nourishment for these seeds, fostering a landscape of mental abundance. Conversely, negative thoughts were the weeds that threatened to choke the garden. Through mindfulness, he uprooted these weeds, replacing them with the vibrant blooms of self-empowerment.

Body and mind converged in harmonious symphony through mindful practices such as yoga and meditation. These practices served as bridges, uniting the physical and the mental in a dance of holistic well-being. Alex's journey through stress and achievement was enriched by the recognition that the mind held the key to nurturing resilience and sustaining mental flourishing.

The Mind-Heart Nexus: Empathy and Self-Compassion

Amidst the academic crescendo, relationships remained a poignant thread in Alex's journey. Professor Evelyn illuminated the significance of empathy and self-compassion – the twin pillars that supported the bridge between the self and others.

By cultivating empathy, Alex traversed the emotional landscapes of others with open-hearted presence. He recognized that understanding another's struggles was not an act of bearing His burdens, but a gesture of sharing the journey. This empathetic connection, woven into the tapestry of His relationships, fostered a sense of belonging and a community of support.

Self-compassion, in turn, was the balm that soothed the wounds of self-critique and perfectionism. Through mindful acknowledgment of His own imperfections, Alex granted himself the gift of self-love. In moments of distress, he whispered words of comfort to himself, rewriting the narrative of self-judgment with the ink of self-compassion.

Empowerment through Vulnerability: The Gift of Authenticity

As the sun neared the horizon, casting a warm glow over the campus, Alex uncovered the transformative power of vulnerability. Guided by Professor Evelyn's wisdom, he learned that vulnerability was not weakness, but an embodiment of courage.

In sharing his journey through mindfulness, Alex opened a window into His soul, inviting others to witness His challenges and triumphs. Through this authenticity, he not only embraced His own vulnerability but also encouraged others to do the same. Vulnerability became a tapestry of connection, woven with threads of shared experiences and shared growth.

Pearl of Insight from Professor Evelyn: In a discourse reminiscent of a gentle breeze, Professor Evelyn shared reflections on vulnerability. "Alex," he affirmed, "authenticity is a beacon that guides you to your own strength. By embracing vulnerability, you empower yourself and inspire others to do the same. Your story is a testament to the beauty of imperfection."

Key Lessons from Chapter 7:

    a. Resilience is nurtured through acknowledging vulnerability and navigating challenges with mindful awareness.

    b. Mindful practices like breathing and self-compassion serve as anchors in emotional landscapes.

    c. The mind-body connection is nurtured through positive thoughts, mindfulness, and holistic practices.

    d. Empathy and self-compassion are twin pillars that strengthen relationships and self-love.

    e. Vulnerability is not weakness; it is a gateway to authenticity, empowerment, and shared growth.

Action Steps:

a. Embrace challenges with mindful awareness, acknowledging emotions without judgment.

b. Practice positive affirmations and self-compassion to nurture a garden of mental flourishing.

c. Engage in mindful practices like yoga and meditation to harmonize the mind and body.

d. Cultivate empathy by being present with others' emotions, fostering connections.

e. Embrace vulnerability as a wellspring of authenticity and shared growth.

As the sun dipped beneath the horizon, painting the sky with hues of serenity, Alex carried himself with the wisdom of resilience and mental flourishing. In the garden of His inner landscape, he nurtured the seeds of strength, tended to the blooms of self-compassion, and wove threads of empathy and authenticity into His tapestry of relationships. The journey through Crestmont University was not just an academic pursuit; it was a profound exploration of the self, illuminated by the torch of mindfulness and guided by the mentorship of Professor Evelyn.

Chapter 8: Navigating Interpersonal Bonds with Mindful Poise

Intertwined Relations

The symphony of academic pursuits harmoniously blended with the intricacies of human connections, Alex's odyssey through mindfulness took a fresh and captivating turn. The wisdom imparted by Professor Evelyn had artfully refashioned His perception of stress and achievement, and now, a new frontier beckoned – the realm of relationships.

As the campus reverberated with the vibrations of social interactions, Alex found himself immersed in contemplation of the complex web of connections that enriched His life. Bonds of friendship, family ties, and romantic entanglements – each relationship emerged as a canvas adorned with a spectrum of emotions, while mindfulness provided the brushstroke to navigate these relationships with grace.

The Craft of Attentive Listening

On a sunlit afternoon, Alex positioned himself beneath the wise, ancient tree, delving into the significance of authentic connection. Echoes of Professor Evelyn's wisdom resounded – "Presence holds the key to relationships." Armed with this insight, he embarked on a journey of attentive listening – a practice that elevated mere conversations into profound exchanges of meaning.

Within a bustling café, Alex engaged in a dialogue with Maya, his closest friend. Rather than waiting for his turn to speak, he invested unwavering attention in every word that spilled from Maya's lips. Every nuance of expression, each nuance of emotion, coalesced to form a mosaic he was committed to unraveling. Within this realm of mindful listening, a connection flourished – a connection that surpassed the superficial.

Professor Evelyn's Discourse: In a conversation reminiscent of a melodious duet, Professor Evelyn expounded on the essence of mindful listening. "Alex," he conveyed, "when you listen with your entire being, you honor the presence of the other. You transcend mere words, delving into the emotional undercurrents beneath. Mindful listening is a precious offering that fosters profound bonds."

Compassion and Empathetic Comprehension

As days morphed into weeks, Alex's exploration of mindful relationships led him to the shores of compassion. He came to realize that compassion was not a grand theatrical gesture; rather, it was the gentle acknowledgment of another's sentiments. It was in the quiet moments, the shared glances of support, that compassion blossomed like the petals of a delicate flower.

On an evening shared with Olivia, his sibling, Alex detected shadows of fatigue etched in Olivia's eyes. Rather than proffering solutions, Alex chose to sit beside her, enveloping her in an aura of empathy. Within this unspoken exchange, compassion burgeoned, nurturing a connection that transcended the necessity for spoken words.

Professor Evelyn's Musings: In a dialogue resonating with the rhythm of empathy, Professor Evelyn shared musings on compassion. "Alex," he reflected, "compassion isn't about mending; it's about coexisting. When you extend understanding, you construct a haven for emotions to find solace. Compassion emerges as a bridge that interlaces hearts."

Resilience and the Art of Resolution

As the semester wove its narrative, it brought forth not only moments of joy and camaraderie but also instances of conflict and misunderstanding. Alex came to understand that mindfulness was not a mere companion during tranquil intervals; it was a beacon guiding him through the labyrinthine twists of conflicts.

In a dialogue with Emma, his teammate, tensions simmered. However, rather than plunging into a verbal duel, Alex took a deliberate breath, reminding himself of the power of mindful presence. He listened intently to Emma's grievances without interruption, acknowledging her emotions without casting judgment. Within this sphere of mindfulness, resolution unfurled akin to a blossoming lotus.

Professor Evelyn's Wisdom: In a conversation that felt like a duet of sagacity, Professor Evelyn illuminated the path of conflict resolution. "Alex," he conveyed, "mindful conflict resolution hinges on taming the impulse to react. By listening mindfully and responding consciously, you interrupt the cycle of escalation. You pave the way for resolution to blossom."

The Unveiling of Mindful Relationships

As the pages of the academic year began His final descent, Alex stood at the crossroads of reflection. Mindfulness had intricately woven itself into every facet of His existence – reshaping trials into opportunities, stress into growth, and relationships into profound connections.

Guided by the teachings of Professor Evelyn, Alex had unraveled the threads of mindfulness, weaving them into an intricate tapestry of empowerment. He had unearthed that mindfulness was not just a technique; it was a philosophy for living, a compass that led him through the labyrinthine journey of life.

Key Lessons from Chapter 8:

    a. Mindfulness becomes a beacon for nurturing relationships through presence and connection.

    b. Attentive listening enriches relationships by acknowledging emotions.

    c. Compassion is cultivated through empathetic understanding and shared spaces.

    d. Mindfulness emerges as a guiding light in conflict resolution by subduing reactive tendencies.

Action Steps:

    a. Infuse your conversations with attentive listening, engaging wholeheartedly with the speaker.

b. Foster compassion by extending understanding and support without judgment.

c. Approach conflicts mindfully, responding consciously and proactively.

d. Reflect on the evolution of your relationships, focusing on instances of presence and growth.

Chapter 9: The Expedition Ahead: Mindfulness as an Eternal Companion

Embarking on the Continuation

The pages of education seamlessly merged with the passages of existence, Alex's expedition through mindfulness arrived at its apex. The insights imparted by Professor Evelyn had fused into a mosaic of empowerment, intricately woven into the very fabric of His being. Yet, as one chapter concluded, another unfurled – the chapter of perpetual mindfulness.

Beneath the wise, ancient tree, caressed by the gentle hues of twilight, Alex contemplated the weight of this transition. His academic voyage had been a nurturing cocoon for transformation, and now he stood ready to unfurl His wings, embracing the world with a demeanor steeped in mindful grace.

The Enduring Legacy of Mindful Living

Glancing over the path he had traversed, Alex perceived mindfulness not merely as a tool but as a legacy. His journey encompassing stress, achievements, relationships, and future visions stood as a testament to the transformative might of mindfulness. With each revelation absorbed and each step undertaken, he had carved a legacy of mindful existence.

Professor Evelyn's Reflections: In an exchange reminiscent of a symbolic torch-passing, Professor Evelyn illuminated the concept of a mindful legacy. "Alex," he conveyed, "mindfulness is a cherished legacy you bequeath. Your expedition is not solitary; it becomes an inspiration for others.

By embracing mindfulness, you sow seeds of empowerment that touch lives."

The Ripple Effect of Mindfulness

As semesters rolled by, Alex's journey intersected with the paths of peers, companions, and even strangers. The far-reaching impact of His mindful choices rippled outward, stimulating conversations, evolving perspectives, and orchestrating transformations. His expedition had transitioned into a tapestry, interwoven not solely with personal growth, but with the flourishing of a community.

During a gathering of friends, narratives of Alex's mindful journey were shared. The struggles, epiphanies, and triumphs resonated, kindling a spark of intrigue. Friends voiced His aspirations to commence His own mindful odysseys, cognizant that within the segments of his lives lay the potential for transformative change.

Professor Evelyn's Insights: In a discourse that mirrored the resonance of empowerment, Professor Evelyn reflected on the expansive ripple effect of mindfulness. "Alex," he noted, "your journey serves as a beacon that lights the way for others. Your openness to share, to connect, ignites the flames of inspiration. Through your enduring legacy, you kindle a collective transformation."

A Commencement, Not an End

As the day of graduation inched closer, emotions swirled within Alex akin to a tempestuous sea. The conclusion of His academic expedition was not a cessation; it heralded the commencement of a new phase. The lessons internalized, the relationships cultivated, the insights assimilated — these formed the steppingstones to a future illuminated by mindful grace.

In a heart-to-heart with Professor Evelyn, gratitude was expressed for the guidance and sagacity received. Professor Evelyn's smile mirrored the journey he had undertaken. "Alex," he conveyed, "the conclusion of one chapter is no farewell; it's a beckoning toward the next. The canvas of your life spans wide, and as you navigate its diverse shades, mindfulness shall remain your steadfast companion."

Key Lessons from Chapter 9:

a. Mindfulness becomes a bequest that empowers future generations.

b. The expansive impact of mindfulness touches lives and ignites transformative change.

c. Graduation marks not a terminus, but a fresh inception guided by mindful grace.

Action Steps:

a. Share your mindful voyage, inspiring others to embark on His unique journeys.

b. Recognize the potential to influence lives through mindful choices and insights.

c. Greet life's transitions with the poise of mindfulness, recognizing the voyage's continuity.

Chapter 10: Embracing the Unknown Future with Mindful Certainty

The Horizon of Impossibilities

Now the crossroads of knowledge intersected with the canvas of personal evolution, Alex's expedition through mindfulness reached its zenith. The echoes of Professor Evelyn's sagacity had shepherded him through stress, accomplishments, and human connections, and now, an uncharted terrain lay before him – the future.

As the sun descended, casting a warm embrace upon the campus, Alex positioned himself beneath the wise, ancient tree. The breeze carried a fusion of anticipation and uncertainty, mirroring the path that stretched ahead. His journey was studded with insights, yet the undefined future unfolded like a blank canvas.

The Palette of Mindful Vision

With each exhalation, Alex released his apprehensions about the future, grounding himself firmly in the present instant. His journey paraded before His mind's eye – mindfulness as a compass to navigate stress, a companion to amplify achievement, and a bridge to forge meaningful relationships. Now, in this chapter of his journey, mindfulness was poised to become a guiding beacon of vision.

Professor Evelyn's Revelation: In a dialogue akin to an unveiling of enigmas, Professor Evelyn imparted insights on mindful vision. "Alex," he shared, "mindfulness is not merely a tool for the present; it is a lantern illuminating the path toward the future. By infusing intention and consciousness into your vision, you carve a roadmap for the journey ahead."

The Authority of Intention

As weeks transformed into months, Alex delved into the concept of mindful intention. He grasped that intention was not a mere wish; it was a deliberate channeling of energy. It was through intention that dreams gained momentum, aspirations took the form of goals.

Seated in his sanctuary of solitude, he shut his eyes and conjured images of his future self. Every detail – the ambiance, the emotions, the triumphs – materialized within his mind's canvas. Inhale by inhale, he breathed life into His vision; with every exhalation, he released skepticism.

Professor Evelyn's Discourse: In a conversation that bore the semblance of a purposeful symphony, Professor Evelyn expounded on the significance of intention. "Alex," he intimated, "intention serves as the rudder that steers your course. When you anchor your journey in intention, you forge a trajectory. Mindful intention transcends the realm of desires; it shapes the persona you evolve into on the journey."

The Choreography of Goals and Present Endeavors

Guided by mindful intention, Alex directed His focus toward goals. He comprehended that goals were more than distant mirages; he represented destinations achieved step by step. Mindfulness, which had been His companion during examinations and relationships, now became his accomplice in the pursuit of aspirations.

Seated at his work desk, he laid out a roadmap – a sequence of actionable strides that would pave the way toward His envisioned future. Whether modest or monumental, each stride metamorphosed into a dance with mindfulness. His concentration was riveted on the present endeavor, and with each stride, a surge of fulfillment coursed through him.

Professor Evelyn's Reflection: In a discourse that mirrored a mosaic of sagacity, Professor Evelyn illustrated the synergy of mindfulness and aspirations. "Alex," he articulated, "mindfulness breathes life into your aspirations. By channeling your focus into each stride, you are not solely reaching a destination; you are living the expedition. It's a synthesis of intention and action."

Gateway to Flexibility

As the chapters of his journey unfurled, so did the capricious nature of existence. Plans altered, circumstances mutated, but within the fabric of change, Alex discerned the thread of adaptability. Mindfulness had honed His capability to maneuver through the unknown with an innate grace.

In conversation with a fellow scholar, he exchanged anecdotes of unforeseen shifts in His trajectory. Rather than being fixated on the setbacks, he spotlighted the lessons and prospects that emerged. In this mindful perspective, adversity assumed the role of a mentor, and adaptability was emblematic of His personal growth.

Professor Evelyn's Reflection: In a discourse reminiscent of an embrace of resilience, Professor Evelyn shared insights on adaptability. "Alex," he articulated, "adaptability isn't solely a reaction to change; it's an outlook that metamorphoses challenges into avenues of potential. Mindfulness nurtures your capacity to bend without breaking, to evolve without sacrificing your essence."

The Mindful Mosaic of Tomorrow

As His final year at Crestmont University drew to a close, Alex found himself positioned at the precipice of the enigmatic future. The canvas of opportunities sprawled before him, infused with the tincture of mindful vision, intention, and adaptability. Professor Evelyn's sagacity had bequeathed him a mosaic of empowerment, woven intricately through the threads of mindfulness.

The voyage through mindfulness had materialized as a symphony of transformation – from turmoil to tranquility, from triumph to development, from relationships to profound bonds, and from uncertainty to purpose. Alex had emerged as the architect of His narrative, the artisan of His canvas, and the navigator of His forthcoming chapters of life.

Key Lessons from Chapter 10:

    a.   Mindfulness evolves into a guiding lantern for envisaging the future.

b. Intention infuses aspirations with purpose, paving the way for the expedition ahead.

c. Goals materialize through mindful present actions, each stride symbolizing a micro-journey.

d. Adaptability, nurtured by mindfulness, converts adversities into possibilities.

Action Steps:

a. Craft a vivid portrayal of your future self through mindful intention, concentrating on particulars and sentiments.

b. Deconstruct your objectives into manageable steps, each suffused with mindful attention.

c. Approach changes with mindfulness, extracting lessons and openings from the flux.

d. Reflect on your voyage thus far, amalgamating mindfulness into your blueprint for the future.

Conclusion: The Mindful Voyage-Unleashing Empowerment Through Presence

The Epitome of Wisdom's Culmination

Within the heart of Crestmont University, where the resonance of learning echoed through the corridors of existence, Alex's odyssey through mindfulness reached its zenith. This journey, a tapestry woven with threads of empowerment, transformation, and revelation, stood enriched by the sagacity of Professor Evelyn and the symphony of mindful living that unfolded.

As the last pages of this chapter were turned, Alex stood at the crossroads of introspection. The fabric he had woven contained strands of stress management, achievements, relationships, and future visions, each day an opportunity for empowerment. The insights assimilated, the hurdles surmounted, and the triumphs cherished, all contributed to the harmonious symphony of mindfulness that now resonated within.

The Potency of Present Empowerment

Mindfulness, a gift bestowed by Professor Evelyn, transcended being a mere tool; it had evolved into a way of life. It equipped Alex to navigate stress-laden waters with resilience, ascend the summits of achievement with purpose, forge relationships brimming with depth and empathy, and paint His future with intention. Beyond these dimensions, mindfulness had become the very essence of each breath, heartbeat, and fleeting moment.

Professor Evelyn's Illumination: In a conversation that seemed to echo through eternity, Professor Evelyn shared his reflections on this transformative voyage. "Alex," he conveyed, "mindfulness signifies the empowerment of presence. Across challenges and victories, you have carried the torch of mindful living. Remember, this is not a conclusion; it is a continuation. Your mindfulness journey remains an ever-evolving symphony and keep passing the torch to enlighten others."

Summary: Embrace the Symphony of Empowerment

Amidst the chapters of this odyssey, Alex unearthed invaluable pearls of wisdom that contributed to His empowerment through mindfulness. These lessons, akin to luminous gems, illuminated His path and shepherded His growth:

Key Learnings	Insights Gained
Stress Management	Mindfulness transmutes stress into resilience.
Purposeful Triumph	Mindfulness imbues action with intention.
Nurturing Bonds	Mindful presence deepens connections.
Vision with Intent	Mindful vision steers the journey.
Everyday Mindfulness	Mindfulness enriches ordinary moments.

Challenges and their Overcoming

As with any expedition, the path of mindfulness was not devoid of challenges. Yet, each challenge was a steppingstone for growth, an avenue to deepen practice:

Challenges	Strategies to Overcome
Distractions	Designate specific times and spaces, keep away all distractors.
Impatience	Begin with brief sessions, extend gradually.
Consistency	Utilize reminders and integrate into routines.
Self-Judgment	Practice self-compassion and acceptance.
Future Anxiety	Anchor in the present through mindfulness.

Tracking Progress: Navigating the Ongoing Journey

Embarking on the path of mindfulness does not culminate in a destination; it initiates a lifelong expedition. In this trajectory of mindful presence, you can monitor your progress using the following action tracker:

Applying Techniques	As needed	Rating (1 to 10, with 10 being highest)
Action Step	Frequency	
Morning Rituals	Daily	
Mindful Work Practices	Throughout the day	

Evening Reflections	Every night	
Mindful Moments	Multiple times (min 3)	
Sharing Mindfulness	Weekly	
Applying Techniques	As needed	

Principal Learnings and Action Steps:

1. Mindfulness is a journey of empowerment through present engagement.

2. Core learnings encompass stress resilience, purposeful accomplishment, nurturing bonds, visionary intent, and daily mindful integration.

3. Challenges are gateways to growth and can be surmounted with patience and strategic approaches.

4. Utilize the action tracker to perpetuate mindful engagement in your life.

Recommended Actions:

1. Assimilate core learnings into your daily routine.

2. Confront challenges with mindfulness techniques and patience.

3. Share your mindful expedition to inspire a ripple effect of empowerment.

Tools & Tips

Some valuable tools for personal development, productivity, and mindfulness, drawing inspiration from a rich tapestry of cultural and philosophical traditions. By incorporating these practices into your daily life, you can enhance your well-being, achieve your goals, and foster a deeper sense of presence and purpose.

1.) Mindful breathing
2.) Mindful body scan
3.) Mindful Walk
4.) Time blocking
5.) The Pomodoro Technique
6.) Habit building & Tracker
7.) Emotional mastery
8.) Visualization
9.) Vision Board

1. Mindful Breathing

Step 1:Find a peaceful and quiet place to sit comfortably.

Step 2:Close your eyes and take a few deep, cleansing breaths.

Step 3: Inhale through your nose slowly, counting to four.

Step 4: Exhale through your mouth, counting to six.

Step 5: Focus your attention solely on your breath, bringing your mind back gently if it wanders.

2. Mindful Body Scan

Step 1: Lie down comfortably with your palms facing up, eyes closed.

Step 2: Begin by focusing on your toes. Notice any tension or sensations.

Step 3: Gradually move your awareness up through your legs, torso, arms, and head.

Step 4 As you identify areas of tension, consciously release them with each exhale.

Step 5 Complete the scan and rest in the awareness of your whole body.

3. Mindful Walk

Step 1: Find a serene outdoor location like a park or garden.

Step 2: Begin walking at a slower pace than usual.

Step 3: Pay close attention to the sensation of each step—lifting, moving, and landing.

Step 4: Engage your senses in your surroundings—the sounds, scents, and sights.

Step 5: When your mind wanders, gently redirect your focus to the act of walking.

4. Time Blocking

Step 1: Identify and list your most important tasks.

Step 2: Allocate specific time blocks in your schedule for each task.

Step 3: During these blocks, concentrate solely on the designated task, avoiding distractions.

Step 4: After each block, take a short break for renewal.

Step 5: Use this method to structure your day for increased productivity.

5. The Pomodoro Technique

Step 1: Choose a task you want to work on.

Step 2: Set a timer for 25 minutes (this is one Pomodoro).

Step 3: Work diligently on the task until the timer rings.

Step 4: Take a 5-minute break to relax and recharge.

Step 5: After completing four Pomodoro, take a longer break of 15-30 minutes.

6. Habit Building & Tracker

Step 1: Identify the habit you want to establish.

Step 2: Start with a small, achievable goal.

Step 3: Track your progress daily using a habit tracker.

Step 4: Reward yourself for milestones and consistency.

Step 5: Continuously refine and expand your habits.

7. Emotional Mastery

Step 1: Practice self-awareness to identify your emotions.

Step 2: Accept your emotions without judgment.

Step 3: Explore the root causes and triggers of your emotions.

Step 4: Develop healthy coping strategies like mindfulness and meditation.

Step 5: Cultivate emotional resilience and balance over time.

8. Visualization

Step 1: Find a quiet and comfortable place to sit or lie down.

Step 2: Close your eyes and imagine your desired outcome or goal.

Step 3: Engage all your senses in this mental imagery.

Step 4: Visualize the process and emotions associated with achieving your goal.

Step 5: Use positive visualization regularly to reinforce your aspirations.

9. Vision Board

Step 1: Collect images, words, and symbols that represent your goals.

Step 2: Arrange these elements on a board or in a digital format.

Step 3: Place your vision board where you can see it daily.

Step 4: Spend time visualizing the life you aspire to while looking at the board.

Step 5: Take action steps towards your goals guided by the inspiration from your vision board.

References:

1. "The Bhagavad Gita" translated by Eknath Easwaran

2. "The Yoga Sutras of Patanjali" translated by Swami Satchidananda.

3. "The Art of Happiness" by Dalai Lama and Howard Cutler.

4. "Yoga Nidra" by Swami Satyananda Saraswati.

5. "The Mandala Book" by Lori Bailey Cunningham.

6. "The Heart of Yoga" by T.K.V. Desikachar).

7. "Full Catastrophe Living" by Jon Kabat-Zinn

8. "The Miracle of Mindfulness" by Thich Nhat Hanh

9. "The Art of Living: Vipassana Meditation" by William Hart

10. "The Pomodoro Technique" by Francesco Cirillo

As we now close the curtain on this book, bear in mind that your journey through mindfulness is a symphony in perpetual motion. The legacy you craft, the connections you foster, and the expansion you experience are all motifs interwoven into the tapestry of your existence. May your days be adorned with the brushstrokes of presence, and may your voyage continue to embolden not just yourself, but also those whose lives you touch.

Thank You with a lot of Gratitude

Contact us at: innerpeacewithabhishek@gmail.com